The Marriage That Was Meant to Break Me: But God...

The Marriage That Was Meant to Break Me: But God...

By: Abigail The Warrior Princess

"The Marriage That Was Meant to Break Me: But God..."

Copyright © 2025 (Abigail the Warrior Princess)

All rights reserved. No part of this book may be reproduced, sold, stored in a retrieval system, or transmitted in any form or by any means, electronic, mechanical, recording, or otherwise, without written permission from the author.

Scripture quotations marked (NLT) are taken from the Holy Bible, New Living Translation, copyright © 1996, 2004, 2007 by Tyndale House Foundation and used by permission of Tyndale House Publishers, Inc., Carol Stream, Illinois 60188. All rights reserved. Scripture quotations marked KJV and NIV are taken from the Holy Bible, King James Version (Public Domain).

Published by: New Voice Books LLC

Website: nvpublishingco.com

Cover design by: Halo Creative Services

ISBN: 979-8-9898714-4-5

Printed in the United States of America

Table of Contents

- Dedication
- Foreword
- Introduction
- Chapter One: Have You Noticed My Daughter, Abigail?
- Chapter Two: Married and Lonely
- Chapter Three: Letter to Tamisha
- Chapter Four: I Married My Father...
- Chapter Five: I Gave My Heart to the Wrong Man
- Chapter Six: What The Wilderness Did For Me
- Chapter Seven: He Calls Me His Warrior Princess

DEDICATION

Papa,

Thank you.

You have healed my father wound with this book. You have helped me to see how the pain that I endured is working for my good.

Sonny,

With this book, I honor your memory. I now understand that you loved me the best way you could. This book will show the world that not everyone intentionally chooses to cause pain, but some of us can only give from a limited capacity. Thank you for teaching me that.

Cecil "Sonny T" "Tasha" Scatliffe 8/24/1965-10/13/24

FOREWORD

I am both humbled and honored to be part of this powerful publication. As a wife and the founder of *Wise Wives Build*, I've had the privilege of walking alongside women of wisdom, strength, and resilience, women like Abigail. I've witnessed her journey, her growth, and her unshakable tenacity.

But let's be honest:
How can something that ends save you?
How can what was meant to bring joy bring so much pain?
How can what the world calls your lowest moment become your greatest turning point?

The truth is, there are seasons when life feels like it's falling apart. Yet it's in those very moments that God is often doing His deepest, most transformative work. This book is a living testament to that reality. When we cried out for healing, for clarity, for purpose, He heard us. In His divine wisdom, He used one of the most sacred and personal parts of our lives, our marriages, not to destroy us, but to reshape us, refine us, and ultimately redeem us.

> "And we know that in all things God works for the good of those who love him, who have been called according to his purpose."
> —Romans 8:28 (NIV)

This book isn't just about the complexities of a relationship between two people. It's about the relentless, redemptive love of God. A love that shows up in every silence, every struggle, every breakdown, and every breakthrough. A love that holds us through the fire and brings us out purified.

> "But he knows the way that I take; when he has tested me, I will come forth as gold."
> —Job 23:10 (NIV)

So, whether your marriage is thriving, hanging by a thread, or still a hope in your heart, this book is for you. It's for the wife who feels unseen. The believer who feels forgotten. The woman wondering if God still hears. My prayer is that as you turn these pages, you'll be reminded that God uses everything, even our most painful places, to reveal His purpose. That He doesn't waste pain. That surrender isn't defeat, but divine positioning.

> "He heals the brokenhearted and binds up their wounds."
> —Psalm 147:3 (NIV)

God will use your marriage, not to break you, but to bring you to your knees, not in despair, but in surrender. And it's there, at His feet, that we find our truest identity and the beauty of who He always intended us to be. May this book stir your faith, bring healing to your heart, and remind you: nothing is ever wasted in the hands of a loving God.

With grace and expectancy,
Coach Williams
The Life Tactician

INTRODUCTION

Confessions of the Battle Ready Wife

Marriage did not turn out the way I thought it would. I had many realistic and unrealistic expectations. I desired to be the best wife I could be. The wife God called me to be. I was content in my single season, knowing that God gave me a desire and purpose in marriage. I thought I was so prepared. I gleaned wisdom from everywhere: single and marriage conferences, married friends, and tons of books, podcasts, videos, etc. Don't get me wrong, they prepared me, but only to a certain extent. You can't be too prepared for marriage because some things will only come out when you are married. I am not saying don't get prepared because preparation is necessary. Just keep in mind that preparation does not mean perfection.

I had no clue what God had planned for me. Little did I know the healing journey I would embark on. I heard a pastor say once, "God tricks us into who we marry to heal us." I didn't like it when he said it, but now I see what he meant. I am not saying we don't have a choice in whom we marry; we do. The pastor went on to explain that during the "Honeymoon" phase, we are blinded to see things in our spouses that would later irritate us. The very thing we are attracted to before marriage is the very same thing that gets on our nerves after we say "I do". Ask any married person, and if they are willing to be honest, they will agree.

The point I am trying to make is this: God uses marriage to heal us. In this book, I will share my journey to healing and wholeness. If you are single, I hope you learn the value of inner healing before you say "I do". For my married sisters, I want this book to provide you with wisdom and insight into the obstacles you may face in your marriage. I want this book to be the tool that encourages you to allow the challenges you may face in marriage to become an opportunity to heal. No matter your marital status, I want you to be free, and I pray this book helps you along the way on your journey to wholeness.

After reading this book, I encourage you to see marriage from a different perspective. This will be a challenge for you to see your spouse through different lenses. I want to ignite a fire in you to fight to protect your union at all costs, even if you have not walked down the aisle. The enemy hates marriages, and he especially hates *Kingdom Marriages*. He has waged war against *Kingdom Marriages*; he attacks them by any means necessary. Even before they start.

Marriage is a perfect union created by God. Though it has its challenges, there are great rewards as well. I don't want you to be discouraged by my story. God has written each of our stories. Mine has just begun. Wait until the plot thickens. You may or may not experience similar things, but that doesn't mean your story will be mine. Trust that whatever path God takes you on, it is one you can bear. Although I didn't get everything I expected, I'm confident I'll always have what I need. No matter the season, God always provides what is needed in every season. Knowing what I know now and how everything turned out, I would still say yes. I have many regrets in my life, but getting married is not one of them.

If I had an opportunity to choose another, my decision would be the same. I do not believe I married the wrong man. My choice was mostly based on what God told me (I'll tell you more about that later). I was not forced, nor did I feel like I didn't have another choice. I trusted God, and I made my decision. I stand by my decision. I know some may disagree with my decision, and that's okay. I am not here to please them; my goal is always to please my Heavenly Father above all else, even my husband. I am writing from a healed place.

This book is not to husband bash but to show God's glory even in the midst of pain. What the enemy meant for evil, God worked out for my good. God has a plan for me, it's a plan to prosper and not to harm me. His plans give me hope and a future.

When I started this book, I thought it was meant to show you how God saved my marriage. But it is really the story of how he saved me from me, and how He used a failed marriage to do so. I do not regret getting married. If asked if I had a chance to do it over, would I? I would say yes. There are too many valuable lessons wrapped in the experience to throw it all away. The way God blessed me in this marriage, I am eternally grateful for the five years He graced me. I didn't realize how much I needed to be saved.

I thought marriage was the goal, but this one was just the path through the wilderness to get to the Promise Land. I was asked, "Do you regret fighting for your marriage because it ended in divorce?" Absolutely not. I fought the fight of faith until the very end. No one chooses to fight to lose. The decision to fight isn't always based on whether you will lose or not. The decision is made when you decide it is worth it. I believe marriage is worth fighting for. I do not regret fighting for what I believe in. I have a testimony, and I'm ready to share…God saved me from myself and used my marriage to do it.

CHAPTER ONE

Have You Noticed My Daughter, Abigail?

This is how I imagine the conversation between God and Satan went before the attacks came. In the book of Job, it appears that God just throws Job under the bus. Like, He just decided Job was good for the job. Let me introduce another possible perspective. When God asks a question, it's never because He does not know the answer. He already knows everything. He asked because He already knew Satan's intentions for Job.

The Bible tells us in **1 Peter 5:8** that the enemy seeks to see who he can devour. He sought out Job. Job caught his attention because of his integrity and devotion to God. When we are in the kingdom of darkness, the enemy doesn't care because he's in control. The moment we accept Jesus and are translated into the kingdom of light, we become enemy #1. The attacks come because we are no longer in his kingdom under his control. Operation steal, kill, and destroy is now in full effect.

Knowing what I know now, I can look back over my life and see where the enemy had it out for me. Thanks to the book of Job, there are many new revelations we see that Job was not privy to. There is no mention of Job being in covenant with God but we know we are in a better covenant established on better promises according to **Hebrews 8:6**. Another revelation we see in Job is when he said, "What I feared most has come upon me", **Job 3:25**. God removed His protection and Satan had access to do whatever but take his life. I share these revelations from Job because they help give an illustration as I share my journey. Some things are attacks of the enemy; others are consequences of our actions and/or the actions of others. There are situations where access was granted to the enemy because of something we did or something done in our bloodline.

The point I want to be clear on is that God is not responsible for the bad things that happen; He does, however, allow them. Jesus never promised us a life without trouble. He told us in **John 16:33** that there will be tribulations, but assured us that He has already overcome the world. We are not exempt from trials; it's guaranteed because we live in a fallen world. The word of God does guarantee that things will work out for our good for those who love God and are called according to His purpose, **Romans 8:28**. It also assures us that weapons will form, but they will not prosper, **Isaiah 54:17**. What we see in the story of Job is just that weapons were formed, but they did not prosper.

God knows our beginning from the end. If He allowed it, He will use it. Ultimately, He used Job to pray for his friends, and Job ended up better than he started. What the enemy meant for evil, God turned it around for His GLORY. The enemy has a plan, and his goal is to steal, kill, and destroy. God's plans for us are good. His plans give us hope and a future. The pain had a purpose. The enemy's goal was for it to destroy me, but God used it to benefit the kingdom. At the end of the story, Job understood God in a deeper way. Our trials are opportunities to get to know God in a way we have not known Him before. On this journey, I got to know my Heavenly Father, and now I really know Him. I know Him as my defender, protector, peace, joy, and this is just the beginning. There is so much more of Him to experience. Like Job, I can confidently declare, "I know my redeemer LIVES!"

It is easy to look at the marriage and think God is definitely not in that. But don't be too quick to judge a book by its cover. I know what God told me. I consulted Him along the way. I inquired of the Lord about the potential of our relationship. I will never forget His response. "You know how I lead you, I lead by my Spirit and I lead by my peace." At that moment, I had a flashback of every relationship up until that point, and I realized I had no peace. But this one was different; I had peace. Other visions and confirmations gave me peace to continue on the path to marriage. So much has been revealed now, and looking back, I can see where certain traumas of my past may have guided my decision or opened a door to what was to come. I don't doubt for one moment that I heard His voice.

Like Job, I had opened doors that the enemy could use, and God allowed it because we gave the legal access. No, I didn't marry the wrong man. I can't even tell you one time where God said no. In fact, His exact words were, "I need you to be patient because there are things in you that he is going to need." That's all I needed! I got the green light, and I ran with it. The problem is that, looking back, I didn't ask follow-up questions. I didn't get the strategy in prayer. All I needed was God's yes, or so I thought. I married him by faith. It wasn't because I was so in love; it was because I trusted God. In my ignorance, I walked into the most intense faith battle of my life. God said he would need me. Surely he would be able to see that, right? NO.

Have you read the book of Job? Everyone talks about Job and how righteous he was and how he didn't curse God. They gave the impression that Job didn't complain about his trials. However, about 40 of the 42 books of Job were about him having some choice words about his circumstances. He even cursed the day he was born. His initial response to the trials was that of worship; however, he still had a moment where he was real with his anger. He had questions for God, and so did I. I was Job, and Job was I. When my marriage wasn't meeting my expectations, I felt robbed; I felt like someone had sold me a lie. I couldn't understand why my marriage turned out like this when I got direction from the Lord. My faith took a huge hit. Did I hear God correctly? Was it my flesh, but I thought it was God?

I was absolutely sure I heard His voice. I mean, I am His sheep; a stranger's voice I shall not follow. Right? I felt betrayed by God. I had so many questions, and doubts often flooded my mind. Insecurity kept me bound, and anxiety tormented me daily. This was the beginning of my healing process. Painful yet rewarding. Just like Job, the trial exposed how little I knew, and it brought me closer than I've ever been to God. What I've learned from the story of Job is how God allows us time to sit with our emotions. God helps us process through the pain with wise counsel.

We saw in the book of Job how three of the four friends who came to be with him had a twisted view of what was happening. I could relate because I had a similar experience. Even some of the most well-meaning advice may not always come from a righteous place. Some made me feel like I wasn't hearing from God. They didn't believe God would lead me on this path. For a time, I believed them, and it brought so much confusion to me. I pray that the eyes of their understanding be flooded with the light of His truth. I am confident that what the enemy meant for evil, my Father will work out for my good. Though He slay me, yet I will trust Him.

Job didn't curse God, but he got dangerously close, and so did I. I believed some horrible things about Him. I didn't curse the day I was born, but I felt like God hated me. I understand Elijah's position after his victory on Mount Carmel. The spirit of Jezebel was on assignment to destroy me. I can't tell you how many times I wanted to commit myself to a mental institution. I felt like God was not doing anything about the emotional abuse I was enduring. There would be great victories, but they were always followed by intense torment. Like Job, my spouse added to the trauma. It felt like he was on a personal assignment from the enemy for my demise.

I thought I was being punished. Are my prayers even being heard? I felt trapped in a pit of despair. Some days, I saw no ladder to get out. I refused to give up. One of my favorite quotes by Kenneth W. Hagin: *"I cannot be defeated, and I will not quit."* My prayers changed. Instead of asking to be rescued, I prayed that He wouldn't let the pain go to waste. I stopped looking at my husband as the enemy and realized I was fighting for both of us. He was not in a position to fight for us. Instead of focusing on what he was and wasn't doing, I started looking inward. I had to focus on my plank and not his speck.

I decided to disarm the enemy first within me. You can't try to cast out a spirit from someone when you are in cooperation with the same spirit. You can't combat their pride if you, too, give place to pride in any capacity. I started to partner with the Spirit of God and dismantle every stronghold the enemy left in my mindset. What I experienced is enough for anyone to walk away from their faith. But GOD...Here I am with faith that is stronger than ever. The affliction was good for me. The testing of my faith produced endurance. The marriage brought just the right amount of crushing to produce oil. This oil is valuable; it cost me a lot.

CHAPTER TWO

Married and Lonely

It's painful to admit it, but I was lonelier as a married woman than I was single. This wasn't supposed to be my story. Marriage is supposed to be better, right? I've cried more as a married woman than I did when I was single. "It's not supposed to be like this. What did I do wrong?" I cried. Somehow, I thought I could control the outcome. "I did it right this time; surely it would turn out differently." But it didn't. I asked myself, "What hell did I sell my soul to?" Now, please don't take this the wrong way; God created marriage, and it's perfect. The problem is that we are imperfect people. One thing I can guarantee marriage will do is expose you. It will expose the soul wounds that went untreated, your flaws, and your selfish ways.

I'm not here to scare you away from the beautifully perfect union God created. I am, however, here to be real and raw with you. I will not set false expectations. I cannot tell you if you do this, you will get that. Some lessons can put you in a better position to become the wife God has called you to be.

Loneliness is a feeling. It's different from being alone. You could be in a room full of people or even have someone in your bed and still "feel" lonely. Loneliness happens when there is a lack of connection. This hits home all too well for me. Many may not be willing to admit it, so I'll speak for myself when I say we subconsciously get married to cure loneliness. Even if it wasn't my main goal, deep down, it was an expectation. This reveals one of the biggest disappointments of marriage because there is this expectation that our spouse is going to fill a void. A void, mind you, they were never supposed to fill. I hate to break it to you, but marriage doesn't make you happy. I am not saying you won't be happy in marriage; what I am saying is it's not our spouse's responsibility to make us happy. It's not your responsibility to make your spouse happy. Happiness can come from different things; however, it's not another human being's responsibility to make you happy.

In the journey of marriage, one of the byproducts of the beautiful institution is to bring healing. Yes, God uses marriage to heal us. Many quit the journey too soon and forfeit the healing that the marriage would've provided. On one hand, I understand that the process of healing can be painful. We may think we made a mistake, and God is like, "Nope, I use your differences to initiate change." He uses our spouse as a mirror. We don't always like what we see. Sometimes, instead of dealing with it head-on, some choose to quit. Some can handle it, and some can't. There is no condemnation.

So, my journey started out really lonely. I would like to blame my husband. It's his fault! If he were a better husband, I wouldn't be lonely, right? Wrong. Even if he were the best husband, I would've still battled with loneliness. It's easy to point the finger, but the reality is that it's not his fault. He is not the enemy. He was being used by the enemy, but what the enemy meant for evil, God works out for our good. His actions only triggered what was already there. I'll go as far as to say that if it wasn't for him, it may have gone unnoticed. Remember, I said loneliness comes from a lack of connection. That void no man can fill; only God can. If you lack intimacy with the Father, you will forever be lonely. No marriage will fill that void. No amount of religious activity will fill the void.

I was expecting my husband to do what I wasn't willing to do for myself. I've said it before and will probably say it again. Marriage exposes you. My codependent tendency was exposed. I depended on others to satisfy emotional needs I haven't developed for myself. I put expectations on people that they were incapable of meeting.

I'm an introvert; I have no problem being by myself. However, I lacked a true connection with myself. Although I was alone, I was always occupied with something, i.e., binge-watching shows or doom-scrolling on social media. The more I dug deeper to identify the root of my loneliness, the more I found that I loathed myself. There were parts of myself that I hated. Externally, I didn't hate what I saw. Up until now, I would've never thought I struggled with self-loathing. I don't look in the mirror and complain about what I don't like about myself. I embraced my voluptuousness. Deep down at the core of me, I had an identity crisis. Yes, the loneliness in my marriage exposed my flawed identity.

When I say my identity was flawed, I mean it was broken. When asked about my identity, I would confidently speak about who I am in Christ. The reality is, as much as I wanted to believe that, subconsciously, I didn't believe. I believed it to be true, but somehow, I couldn't accept it for myself, like I was the exception to the rule. It was easier to believe the promises for everyone but myself. The loneliness forced me to confront my double-mindedness.

I would declare the word, but struggle to receive it. It's not that I didn't want to receive it; I just also believed things about myself that contradicted the word. I was so blinded by lies that I didn't even recognize that I was a people pleaser. I so desperately craved validation. I actually thought that because my husband married me, he saw the value in me as his wife. I was wrong. Not only did he not see it, he also rejected it.

I thought being a people pleaser was just doing things to get people to like you. I'm a natural-born leader. I don't do things because someone tells me to. However, I did do whatever was necessary to "prove" my value and worth. No, it did not occur to me that it was the same thing. I didn't even realize that's what I was doing. Marriage was a huge magnifying mirror. I experience loneliness because I was disconnected from my true identity. I had to learn how to accept myself. In the next chapter, I detail my journey of reconnecting to myself.

CHAPTER THREE

Letter to Tamisha

Dear Tammi,

For about two decades, I've abandoned you. Please forgive me. I neglected you as if you were never a part of me. I didn't realize hating the name meant I hated myself. I now realize the detachment from my name had to do with my father, but I rejected you instead. For that, I apologize. Please accept my apology. I didn't hate you, but I hated the name. It never felt like it fit who I was and who I am. You and I are one. Taking on a new name doesn't mean I have to lose a part of me, but that I can walk into the fullness of who I am.

We were rejected and didn't know why. At this point, why he did it is irrelevant. I want to lead you(us) to a place I like to call Promise. Forgive me. I tried to go without you. Promise is a place of freedom, abundance, protection, healing, rejoicing, wholeness, and so much more. Promise is a place for both of us. It's a place where we thrive together! There is this man whose name is Jesus. You've heard His name before, and there are things that you've heard or believe that may not be true. Can I reintroduce you to Him? You will find that you've always known Him; you just didn't realize it was Him.

Promise is a place where we go and where we are at the same time. It's not a place we have to travel far to get to. Many have a hard time getting to it, mostly because they have the wrong guide or they try to guide themselves. It's called Promise because that's where the Promise Keeper lives. He's the Promise Keeper because He keeps ALL His promises! Jesus is the only way to Promise; He is the only one who can get us there. It's a beautiful story. At another time, I'll tell you the full story, but today, I'll share an abridged version just for you.

The Promise Keeper sent His son, Jesus, to be the guide for everyone who wanted to come to the Promise. He sent Jesus on a journey to get to us before He could guide us. Jesus would have to enter the earth as a baby and live just like one of us. Jesus left the riches and comfort of the Promise to come to this world we call earth to live and experience life the way we do. I should tell you that not just anyone can get into Promise. You have to have a seal or proof of authenticity; without it, you can't get in. The reason Jesus is the only guide is because of His sacrifice, which is why we have the seal. Jesus sacrificed His life so that many more can get the seal to get in. When you accept His sacrifice on your behalf, you get the seal. That's it! You don't have to do anything but believe in Jesus.

When we believe in Jesus, we trust Him to lead us to Promise. We also trust Him to continue to guide us in every area of our lives. This is very important. There are things we hold onto that are not allowed in Promise. Some may be small, others are big; either way, they hinder our journey to Promise. Many don't make it into Promise because they refuse to let those things go. I want you to go to Promise with me. Together, you and I will have to let some things go.

We will have to go back to places we swore we wouldn't go back to. Know this: We will not be alone. We have Jesus, and He will go with us. And you remember when I said you may realize He was always there? This is an opportunity for Him to show us. I'm not going to say it will be easy and painless. I'm not going to lie, it will be hard, and it will hurt, but guess what? Jesus is a healer! He can heal any wound as if it never happened. He is from Promise, and He keeps His promises.

Are you ready? Where should we begin? Let's start with the earliest memory of rejection. I don't remember our age exactly, maybe 3 or 4. Do you remember being excited to see your dad? You knew he was your father, but you called him Sonny. He was away often, so this particular day, you were excited to see him. Without even thinking, you screamed out, "Daddy, Daddy!" and He raised his hand to hit you. You didn't mean to make him angry with you. You always call him Sonny. What came over you? Right there, let that go.

You did nothing wrong; this was not your fault. It's not your responsibility to manage others' emotions. His inability to regulate his own emotions has nothing to do with you. We wouldn't've noticed it right then, but a plan was already in place to redeem you. I'll share more about that later. Years after this occurrence, one of your sisters was over at the house to visit, and she called out to him, "Daddy, Daddy!" You flinched, and it took you back to that day. You thought he would respond the same way he did to you, and HE DIDN'T! Why did I get scolded, and she didn't? What's wrong with me? Right there, that's it. At this moment, you probably felt rejected, and I believe this is where the self-loathing program was installed.

A program is installed in our belief system; a negative program is installed when any form of trauma occurs. This is where you first believed the lie that you were not enough. The reality is that him not wanting you to call him "Daddy" had nothing to do with you and everything to do with him. He doesn't even call his mother "Mom". Whatever his reason, we can now let him go. Forgive and release every emotion associated with this experience. The name change was strategic; it's a correction to this experience.

Jesus, mend every wound created by this experience, and allow us to see You in this experience.

I see that day differently now. I see my excitement to see my father, and I'm embraced so lovingly by Jesus. He was happy to see me, and he's always happy to see me. Every time I hear my name, it's a reminder of his excitement for me! No one can take that from me. Abigail means father rejoices. Yes, you got it! The new name wasn't to replace you; it was to redeem you.

But now, thus says the Lord, who created you, O Tamisha, And He who formed you, O Abigail: "Fear not, for I have redeemed you; I have called you by your name; You are Mine. (Referenced Isa 43:1)

Tamisha, you are redeemed; you are your father's joy; you are Abigail. Every time you come into His presence, He rejoices. He loves it when you take time to spend with Him. You don't have to be afraid to approach Him. If you were the only one, the Promise Keeper would've sent Jesus just for you. You are valuable to Him. How do you feel now? Do you see how this journey is worth it? Don't you feel so much better already? And this is only the beginning.

I have to tell you, I'm so glad we are on this journey together. I have to apologize to you again. Not only did I abandon you, but I also realized that I've rejected and hated you. I always treated you as if you were weird or abnormal. I always felt like something was wrong with you. I tried so hard to make you fit into a box, one that you were never meant to fit. I took your differences as something was wrong, but different doesn't mean bad. The Promise Keeper made every one of us different on purpose. He said we are fearfully and wonderfully made. So, some of the things you do aren't because you are faulty, but because you were uniquely designed that way.

Due to a lack of understanding, you were mishandled. I am so sorry. I wish I had known sooner. I wish they knew, but we didn't know, none of us did. There are so many who realize this information later in life. The more I understand neurodivergence, the more everything makes sense. You were never meant to be typical. I want to free you today. It's okay to be different. The challenges you've had aren't because you are defective. Nothing is wrong with you! You are ENOUGH! I want you to forgive me.

I want you to forgive our parents and family. I want you to forgive every person who has mishandled you. We didn't know or understand. Now I do, and moving forward, I will do a better job of advocating for you. People will always mistreat what they don't understand. I can't speak for everyone, but I know if our family had understood what we know now, things would've been different. So, give them grace for what they didn't know. Just as Jesus said, "Father, forgive them for they know not what they do." There are many experiences I wish we could go over, but there's not enough time. There are a few things I do want to address.

ONE: YOU ARE NOT LAZY!

I break that word curse from over you. You likely have what they call PDA, which is a common trait in neurodivergent individuals. Pathological Demand Avoidance causes you to struggle with some basic tasks or commands. There are so many things that I am realizing that were once considered "weird" are linked to neurodivergence. The picky eating, the sensory overload, and the missed social cues. I'm thankful for the language that we now have. The focus is no longer on changing you but on embracing your strengths and managing your weaknesses. The Promise Keeper is the creator. He created you this way. His power works best in our weaknesses. We can always look to Him for wisdom and understanding of how He created us to function. You are special by design. You were created for good works. We just need to learn about them and understand them.

Jesus, you know us better than we know ourselves. Help us to understand how and why you created us. Give us wisdom on how to accept and manage our unique qualities. May we see every weak area as an opportunity for your power to manifest in our lives.

TWO: YOU ARE NOT TOO SENSITIVE

You are neurodivergent, which means your nervous system is wired differently, which may cause your senses to be more stimulated easily. You are more sensitive than some, but it's not your fault. You can't control it. Let's talk about our emotions. We grew up with very little understanding of our emotions and how to manage them. The reality is that we experience some levels of emotional trauma, abuse, and neglect. We were taught incorrectly how to deal with our emotions. The message that was given was either that what you feel doesn't matter, or that you were bad for feeling what you feel. Today, we are dismantling those lies. I release you from the prison of shame. Your emotions are nothing to be ashamed of.

Emotions are the alarm system of our soul. They tell us what is happening, and they should always be trusted. Your emotions don't define who you are. Now, your feelings are not the same thing as emotions. Feelings are an interpretation of the emotions you experience. The interpretation may be based on the truth, a fact, or a lie. On this journey, we will uncover the source of some of the feelings we've had. This will be uncomfortable. We will go back to some traumatic experiences, and we will experience some emotions. But this time, we will process through them. By the end of the journey, we will be well on our way to being emotionally healthy and mature.

Jesus, we cast every care, every emotion to you. Heal every wound that left an emotional scar in our souls. You are near to the broken-hearted, and you restore our souls. Restore every broken, fractured, empty space in our souls. Remove every unnecessary memory attached to emotional trauma. Thank you.

THREE: YOU CAN SING

Our next stop should be to get our voice back. The Promise Keeper gives us certain gifts or talents; one of ours is singing. Do you remember when you first realized you loved to sing? I don't, either. I do remember always feeling like I'm not a good enough singer. Probably didn't help that our family wasn't encouraging or affirming our gift, which may have worked for our good. Although it would've been nice to know that they like to hear you sing. We started singing in elementary school, and we were in the school choir. Christmas time was the best because singing carols brought so much joy. Looking back and knowing what I know now, it makes so much sense why we had a variety of music styles. So much so that our voice had a unique sound. It made us stand out in a way that warranted unnecessary criticism. Do you remember?

It was our 6th-grade promotional exercise, and we sang a duet. I vaguely remember the song because I suppressed the memory. You were so nervous about having to sing in front of so many people. Only to overhear some classmates criticizing your sound. That experience broke something in us. It fractured our confidence in the gift we were given. Many other instances further damaged or chipped away at what little confidence was left. Finally, by the time we made it to high school, we vowed never to sing again unless it was for the Lord. Do you remember? We had no idea that we were creating an inner vow. We came into an agreement with a lie. What may seem like a noble gesture was a trap to keep our voice hidden unnecessarily. The Promise Keeper didn't want to keep our voice to himself. He meant for it to be shared; to set captives FREE!

We have to come out of agreement with this lie, say this with me: *" I renounce the vow that I will never sing again unless it is for the LORD. I desire for my voice to be heard wherever the LORD wills. I am His mouthpiece, and those who have ears to hear what He is saying through me will hear it. LORD, break the power of this vow over my life. I come into agreement with Ephesians 2:10, I was created for good works. The plans He has for my voice, I will walk into them."*

Let's talk about it. We have carried the weight of shame for far too long. The Promise Keeper has an enemy, and he does every and anything he can to stop as many people as possible from going to the Promise. His name is the Accuser. He always tries to destroy the Promise Keepers' plans. Here's what I believe happened. Promise Keeper gave us a unique sound. One that many people don't understand or recognize. The Accuser used people to reject the sound. The rejection caused us to think we didn't have a gift. We walked around thinking we couldn't do the very thing we were graced to do. It developed a shame so deeply rooted that we buried the gift.

Remember, I said what people don't understand, they mishandle. The reality is that the Promise Keeper gave us a new sound because He could trust us with it. Not many are trusted with this sound. Our gift was mishandled because many didn't recognize it. When people didn't recognize it, shame set in, and we thought we were not good enough. Those who have an ear to hear will recognize our unique sound. It worked out that some didn't recognize it, as it prevented many from abusing the gift. We have a prophetic voice, a unique sound. A sound that set captives free. I break the power of shame and lose its control over our voice.

Jesus, forgive us for every time we mishandled the gift. Every time we allowed fear and shame to keep us from flowing in the gift you have given. Help us to understand the gift and the purpose so we will no longer misuse it. Restore back every time and opportunity missed because of fear.

Abigail, I forgive you. Thank you for coming back for me. I feel so much lighter and hopeful. I'm so grateful you've introduced me to Jesus. I look forward to our journey to Promise. Every time I release and forgive, I feel like I'm floating because I'm no longer holding onto the pain and resentment. I don't have to hold those things anymore; I can give them to Jesus!

Tamisha, thank you for trusting me. I know in the past I didn't deserve your trust. From now on, I promise you I will value you more. I still have a lot to learn, but I am committed to being more compassionate and kind to you. Your well-being is my first priority. I am dedicated to showing you grace, NO MORE SHAME. Promise, here we come.

CHAPTER FOUR

I Married My Father...

It was very hard for me to accept this reality. To make it even worse, less than a week after I titled this chapter, my father was murdered. It's no surprise I had daddy issues. I just didn't realize how much it affected my life choices. I just wanted to be loved and accepted. Oftentimes, we neglect to see how much childhood trauma we have and how it affects our lives. It's mostly subconscious, where we don't realize it until it's pointed out. I'm not here to point the finger at my father; I'm acknowledging the insecurities that were birthed from our broken relationship. What I yearned for from my husband was really what I wanted from my father. When I realized that I couldn't get what I needed from my father, my next goal was my husband.

The reality is that both men were broken and could not give me what I truly needed. The obvious answer is our Heavenly

Father, right? Well, it took me some time to truly receive the all-powerful God as Father. I couldn't receive God as Father because I was projecting my natural father onto my Heavenly Father. In many ways, I couldn't trust God to come through because I've been let down so many times. I see things differently now, but at one point, I felt like God had let me down with this marriage. I was rejected and abandoned as a child, and without trying, I ended up in a marriage where I was rejected and abandoned.

Looking back, I realized a lot of what I experienced in the marriage was like deja vu. I would do whatever I could to gain acceptance, like learn to cook meals they like. Silent treatment was the worst. Silence always means they are angry, and I would have to question what I did now. In the marriage, it always felt like nothing I did was enough. In many ways, I would prove my love, but it was never enough. Can you tell if I'm talking about separate people or the same person? It was separate people but the same familiar spirit.

There is only one to blame, and that's the enemy. Neither my father nor my spouse was the enemy. **John 10:10** tells us **the thief comes to steal, kill, and destroy**. It would be easy to label the men in my life who failed me as villains. We were all victimized, and they were pawns in the enemy's game set to destroy me. What the enemy meant for evil, God strategically uses for His Glory.

If I can only choose one thing that this book will impart to you, it is this: "CAPACITY". Capacity is defined as *the maximum amount or number that can be contained or accommodated*. We all have different levels of capacity. **Romans 12:3** mentions that we each were given a measure of faith. In context, the author is encouraging us to be mindful of our abilities and stay within the limits that were given by God.

Do you know what your capacity is? Are you able to measure what another's capacity is? There will be less disappointment when you understand one's capacity. I understand now that my husband did not have the capacity to be the husband I needed. Actually, he didn't want to. He rejected the opportunity to become the husband I needed. It was his right; he has free will. Lack of understanding leads to deception…always. The enemy can deceive us when we don't understand. He was able to deceive Eve, who did not understand her identity. And he deceived me of my identity and my father's love.

The things that I needed from my father that I didn't get, I thought it was because he didn't want to give them to me. There is a difference between can't and won't. I thought my father was making a choice not to do and be what I needed.

This is where understanding one's capacity will impact how you view the person and the situation. I was expecting more from him than he had to give. I now believe that whatever my father didn't do was not because he didn't want to. If he had the capacity to do it, I believe he would've. One of the best memories I have of my father is of a particular time when I thought he was not going to show up for me. I was in a pageant, and I had lost. My family came to congratulate me, but the moment I saw my father, I broke down crying. At that moment, though I lost, I felt like a winner because my father was there.

I remember one of the last memories I have with my father. I have to admit, at that moment, I mocked it, but didn't realize how much I needed to experience that moment. My father had been battling with his mental health for years. What seemed like a moment of him saying something crazy will now be a moment I will never forget. At the time, I disregarded the exchange of him talking to himself; now, I understand the Lord allowed me to witness the battle he was going through. When my father saw me, it was as if he were having a conversation with someone who wasn't there. He said, "That is my firstborn, my pride and joy." What I thought was a random "crazy" moment was him fighting the best way he could to express how he felt about me. I can't remember a time when I heard my father talk about me like that. That's the last memory I have, and for that, I am thankful. My father loved me to the capacity that he had, and it was enough.

I hate that it took my father being murdered, a life senselessly stolen, for me to get this revelation. I'm angry that I don't have the opportunity to share this with my father. I will make the enemy pay for what he stole from me. My life will be lived not just in honor of my Heavenly Father but also in honor of my earthly father as well. As long as I'm on this earth, his life will not be in vain.

CHAPTER FIVE

I Gave My Heart to the Wrong Man

My father was the first man to break my heart. Somewhere deep down, I decided to withhold my heart from him and give it to another. It's funny how our minds choose to remember certain things and not others. Now, looking back, I am reminded of a particular time when my father warned me. Or at least he did it in the best way he knew how. At the time, I rejected it because I felt it was a little too late, or maybe it was my teenage self thinking I knew everything. My father warned me about the boy who would eventually rape me. At the time, I didn't see it because it was the first boy who paid attention to me and desired me.

This is the first time that I'm publicly acknowledging that I was raped. It took me decades to realize that it was rape. I thought I was going to hang out with some friends, but he had other plans for me. Sex was never on my mind. I thought he just wanted to spend time and get to know me, but I was wrong. I said no, and he didn't care, and he took something valuable from me. And then he discarded me like trash, acting like he never knew me a day in his life.

I gave my heart to the wrong man, and he would be the first of many, unfortunately. Each guy was different, and yet they were all the same. For years, it was an endless cycle of situationships. I realized that I was the common denominator. I was settling for what they were willing to offer. And I wanted more.

I barely understood my value, yet I hoped they would finally see. Then I figured that the one who is willing to marry me, surely, he will see it. So, I waited for "The ONE". I prepared for "The ONE"; instead, I should have become "The ONE" first. Don't get me wrong, preparation is not bad. We have to have balance, and I did not. Preparing for the one and becoming the one are two separate experiences. I was focused more on preparing, not becoming.

My entire life up until this point, I have been searching for the one that I can give my heart to, the one that could take care of it, the one that I could trust my heart to, but it was never for me to give away. **Proverbs 4:23** states **Above all else, guard your heart, for everything you do flows from it.** It's my responsibility to guard my heart and not to find someone to give it to. To guard requires you to supervise what comes in and out. I had to repent of this faulty thinking. I do need to be selective with those that I trust my heart to, but that doesn't mean I give it to them. The last man I gave my heart to crushed it. He rejected, abandoned, and disregarded my heart as nothing. Praise God, he heals the brokenhearted and binds up their wounds.

The reality is, I abandoned my heart long before he did. I was looking for a man to do what I needed to do for myself. I didn't trust myself with my own heart. I was careless with my heart. We mishandle what we don't understand. Lack of understanding, or should I say, leaning on your own understanding, always leads to deception. The enemy can deceive us when we don't fully understand.

Eve didn't understand her identity and that she was already made in the image of God. She already had god-like qualities. When we don't understand our purpose or calling, our weaknesses, and our strengths, we become easy prey for the enemy. I didn't understand how much my father loved me with the limited resources that he had. For most of my life, I believed that my father didn't care. It pains my heart to now realize how wrong I was.

Praise God again for the reminder that he heals the brokenhearted and binds up their wounds! Rejection is a wound that, when left unattended, grows and sometimes gets deeper with time. Oftentimes, when rejected, our response is to reciprocate rejection. We build up walls meant to protect us, not realizing the walls also keep others out; NO ONE can get in. I built up a wall intended to protect myself, and in the process, my heart hardened. Yet, still yearning to be loved and accepted, inadvertently in the process, I was blocking out and was unable to receive the love that I truly needed. I didn't realize that the wall I built was rejecting God's access. The wound of rejection had cut so deep that I was rejecting the very thing I wanted.

Remember, a lack of understanding always leads to deception. "And in all you're getting get understanding", Proverbs 4:7.

I now understand that the rejection that I received from my father was just a mirror of the rejection of himself and a mirror of the rejection from his father. It's a perpetual cycle of rejection. A generational cycle of trauma of rejection. And it stops with me. I now understand that the rejection that I received from my husband had little to do with me, but more to do with his rejection of himself. The rejection that he received from others is yet another cycle of rejection that keeps perpetuating itself until properly dealt with.

I now understand that I am truly chosen and accepted, and I shall no longer fall prey to rejection because I am fearfully and wonderfully made. I was created for a purpose, with a purpose on purpose. I am anointed to set captives free, and I am fiercely loved. I now understand the value and importance of my relationship with myself. The affliction was good for me. He used the very man who broke my heart to heal me. I'm in awe of His greatness. What the enemy meant for evil, God is using for His glory. This is the epitome of beauty for ashes.

CHAPTER SIX

What The Wilderness Did for Me

When you think of the word "wilderness," what comes to mind? Wasteland, barren, uninhabited, and neglected are some words that were used to describe a wilderness. So, it's natural for one to think that the wilderness is a bad place to be. With that being said, how do you deal with the fact that God led you to the wilderness? I know what you're thinking: Why would He? God wouldn't do that! Really? Ask Jesus about that; see (**Matthew 4:1**) if you think I'm lying. Then read the story in Exodus of how God led His chosen people out of slavery to the Promise Land, but first...they had to go through the wilderness. What should've been an 11-day journey turned into a 40-year-long wandering. God's ways and thoughts are far higher than ours; He uses the foolish things to confound the wise.

The place of your greatest weakness can be the same place of your greatest victory. God didn't lead the Israelites or Jesus to die; He led them to victory. How you respond in the wilderness will determine how long you stay in the wilderness. It's easy to read the story in Exodus and judge the Israelites. They saw God move so mightily on their behalf, then they got to the wilderness and doubted Him. Don't be too quick to cast judgment on how others are handling a season, because what you judge, you may be guilty of. I remember judging the Israelites until I walked through my wilderness season. The marriage was my wilderness experience.

There was a long period of waiting. Although I didn't regard my single season as a slavery experience like some do, it was long. Then the word came: a prophecy, "Your husband is coming soon. It will be a quick process, and it will be a God thing. You both will be in ministry together." My spirit leaped for joy, not so much because my husband was coming but because we would be in ministry together. It was confirmation of something I always sensed but never shared with anyone. Shortly after, my husband came on the scene, and I inquired of the Lord about him. His response to me was, "You know how I lead you, I lead you by my Spirit, I lead you by my peace." Instantly, He reminded me of every other "situation-ship" where there was no peace. This time, I had peace.

So here we are. The Lord made a promise, and He led us out of Egypt. What's next? The Promised Land? Not quite...but first the wilderness. Like the Israelites, I couldn't see what God was doing in the wilderness. I was so distracted by what I wasn't getting. Marriage didn't feel like a blessing, but HELL! I remember crying, "What hell did I just sell my soul to?" I missed my single season; it wasn't always fun, but I was good. I've cried more in my marriage than I did in my 9 years of being single. It wasn't supposed to be like this! I waited!

I couldn't understand why God would bring me this way. I started to feel like I had done something wrong. I felt like I was being punished. I was so sure that God led me this way, but I had a hard time understanding why He would lead me this way if He knew it would turn out like this. Trust was broken, and my faith was challenged.

Just like the Israelites, I murmured and complained. This was not what I expected. I expected the land of milk and honey. Isn't that what marriage is supposed to be? To answer the question, yes. However, I forgot about the journey through the wilderness. And to be fair, even once they got to the Promise Land, they still had to fight and contend for what was theirs. They are still fighting to this day. We will always have to fight to protect our promise. Always fight to protect your marriage. Facing challenges and obstacles in your marriage does not mean you married the wrong person. (Disclaimer: I am not referring to any form of abuse.)

I thought I made a mistake. Maybe I thought I heard God, but I was wrong. Clearly, everyone thought I made a mistake. A husband is supposed to love, provide, and protect. Many times, I wasn't even getting the bare minimum. How could this be God's will? God's methods and ways are infinite; don't be too quick to judge. God always has a strategy. Oftentimes, we may not understand until the end.

I did not realize Egypt was still in me. I was out physically, but it was still in me. The wilderness exposed what I couldn't see. I couldn't see that I was still a slave when I was called to be a child. What I thought was punishment was actually exposing what God wanted out of me. The wilderness exposed that I was still operating as an orphan. I was not secure in my identity. I thought I was, but I wasn't. God freed me from Egypt, but He saved me in the wilderness.

There was a different route God could have used to take the Israelites to the Promise Land. It was shorter and easier. However, the route He chose was on purpose. He knew what they would be faced with ahead, and the shorter route would not have prepared them. The wilderness route presented some challenges that would train and prepare them to dominate when they arrived in the Promise Land.

They were trained in the art of war, and they learned to trust in the Lord's provision and protection. For some, the wilderness provided an opportunity for intimacy with the living God. Only a few took advantage of that opportunity. Moses experienced His Glory. Joshua got closer than anyone else did. He would become their next leader and lead them into the Promise Land. Caleb, along with Joshua, was able to focus on the power of God, rather than the power of the enemy, unlike the other spies.

Moses, though he was able to be the closest to God, was unable to enter the Promise Land. He allowed the people to frustrate him, which caused him to disobey God. In the wilderness, it is important not to get distracted. It is easy to lose sight when obstacles and challenges fight to gain your attention. Like Moses, there were times when I allowed myself to be distracted by what was being said and done to me. In those moments, I may have missed some key instructions. I was, however, able to see how the enemy was using these things against me. Once I shifted my perspective and saw each obstacle as an opportunity for me to experience the living God in a way I've never experienced before. Every obstacle became a lesson.

What did the wilderness do for me? In the wilderness, I was trained in the art of war. It was the right training ground for a prayer warrior. I learned how to trust in His provision and protection. It drew me closer to Him more than ever before. I encountered His mercy and became acquainted with His grace. I understood my identity and purpose. I knew my identity, but there were aspects that I didn't understand. I do now. I'm glad He chose this route for me. I am wiser and stronger because of the wilderness. It was good for me that I was afflicted, for it taught me your ways. (**Ps. 119:71**)

CHAPTER SEVEN

He Calls Me His Warrior Princess

They went into the wilderness as slaves, but they entered the Promise Land as Warriors. The marriage challenged my relationship with the Father. He saved me from myself, and He used this marriage to do it. He allowed me to enter into a toxic marriage. Not to punish me but to save me. The Israelites thought they were being punished in the wilderness, but God was saving them. This is my story, not yours. No, I'm not saying He will do the same thing to you. This wilderness the Lord led me to; I will leave victorious.

I've learned not to question God's sovereignty. Now, I don't mean we can't ask questions, I mean questioning His motives. We don't even know our hearts at times, yet we want to judge God's? Couldn't He use a different way to heal? Of course, but it had to happen this way, and I trust if He allowed it, He will use it. I'm not telling you I never questioned God's motives or never doubted His plan. I did, but I am on the other side, telling you it's worth it. The times when I didn't understand now make so much sense. Right now, you may not understand, and that's ok. I promise it will be clearer the more you focus on Him and who He is. The more you focus and concentrate on the circumstances, the more confusing it will be.

Was this marriage in God's plan for me? I would say yes. Even though it ended in divorce, it doesn't mean it wasn't God's plan. We often quote **Jeremiah 29:11** to a T. "I know the plans and thoughts I have for you...Plans to prosper you, not to harm you, plans of peace, not evil, to give you a future and hope." If you read a few verses above at the beginning of the letter, He addresses those who have been taken captive, and says, "Whom I have caused to be carried away." Yet He told them my thoughts and plans are good. God didn't promise us a life of perfection; His thoughts and plans didn't mean it would be sunshine, rainbows, and candy. We incorrectly interpret that scripture to mean everything will be rose colored and cute and aesthetically pleasing. So, when I look back on my decision and why I made it, I know unequivocally that the Lord led me here.

Remember, what caused them to be captured was their disobedience. I'm not saying God led me to a toxic marriage because that was His best for me. I can acknowledge my trauma and insecurities that influenced my decisions. The marriage was a consequence of my idolatry. Idolatry can be subtle; it's not just you bowing to carved images, it's anything that you fear more than God. I feared man's opinion of me more than God's opinion. I hate to admit it now, but that was my reality. It was as if what He said about me was not enough.

I was trying to prove my worth to those who couldn't recognize or afford my value. I shrink myself to make others comfortable in their insecurity. Subconsciously, I thought being married would increase my value. I wasn't secure in my value; I didn't understand my value. My value was determined before I was even born by the Creator, my Father, and there is nothing that can add or take away from it. My worth is fixed by God; eternal, priceless, and beyond debate.

God led me to the marriage, not because it was His perfect will but because of my ignorance. This was His permissive will because He wanted to use it, and that He did. Thank God for His mercy towards me. His power is perfected in our weakness; His grace was sufficient for me. And now I see that it was for my good. Was it always fun? No, but the marriage did something for me that I'm eternally grateful for; it put me on this healing journey that I didn't know I needed. God blessed me in this marriage. He saved me from myself, and He developed me into a WARRIOR.

Before marriage, I thought I knew who I was. I was confident in my identity. The wilderness did so much for me. I found the missing piece to my identity. I didn't realize it was missing. The wilderness will do that to you; it exposes what was hidden or missing. Realizing my neurodivergence filled in so many missing pieces. God gave me a different way to see HIS world. Understanding autism has literally unlocked me from a mental prison I've been in my entire life. Now that I understand myself better, I can handle myself better. Here I was trying to fit into a box I was never designed to fit in.

The journey through the wilderness was one of self-discovery, self-acceptance, and self-worth. I went in bold but came out even bolder. I went in as a captive, but I came out a warrior. It was on this journey that I learned I am His Warrior Princess. He uses me as a battle axe in the spirit. I feel more loved by God than I've ever felt. What I thought was meant to break me only trained me. What's a Battle Ready Wife without a battle?

As a generational curse breaker in my family, I thought my marriage was supposed to be a symbol of hope. I was the first one married, and my marriage was supposed to be a symbol of a godly marriage, right? Instead, it was more like a crash course on trauma 101. Despite that, I believe that the marriage still taught me plenty. I thought the breaking of the curse was to have a successful marriage. It would seem as if I failed miserably. I did not. Actually, I passed with flying colors. The wilderness was a test. I entered into a covenant, not just with a man, but also with God. And despite the obstacles and opportunities, I kept my covenant. I kept my covenant when I had all the reasons not to. And the curse was broken.

God honored me for keeping my covenant by allowing my daughter to be married to a man who loves and cherishes her. As a mother, it pleases your heart to know that your child will not have to go through what you did. She is doing far more and is in a far better place than I was at her age. I did something right. The cycle is broken. I need you to understand the miracle that is in my family.

My daughter witnessed both her parents' failed marriages. She's seen enough to swear off ever being married. At her age, being married is very uncommon in our culture. He gave me beauty for ashes. To be able to witness the fruits of my obedience is such a pleasant reward. My heart is filled with joy every time I see them together. If I went through all of that to bring us here? It was all worth it. The affliction was good for me.

When I first started writing this book, I didn't expect we would be where we are now. I thought we were meant to go into the Promise Land together; he chose not to. For the time that I was allowed, I'm honored to be his wife. I'm beyond thankful for him. Some may see this as a failure, but the greatest lessons are found in failure. However, I don't view this as a failure. I accomplished all that I was assigned to do, and I gained great lessons and wisdom in the process. The enemy would try to make me feel like I'm a failure as a wife, but I know I am a better wife because of this experience. My marriage was not restored, but I was. I didn't get marriage restoration; I got restoration in marriage. I am even more determined now, more than ever, to bring healing and deliverance to Kingdom Marriages, one wife at a time.

Allow me to reintroduce myself. I am Abigail, the Warrior Princess. He calls me His Warrior Princess. I created Battle Ready Wives to empower ALL WIVES. The Married Wife, Never Married Wife, Divorced Wife, and Widowed Wife. I have a mandate from Heaven, and the assignment is clear. As His battle axe and weapon of war filled with His wisdom, I not only destroy kingdoms, I also destroy strongholds and release breakthrough. I am in the business of setting captives FREE!

www.ingramcontent.com/pod-product-compliance
Lightning Source LLC
Chambersburg PA
CBHW070107100426
42743CB00012B/2679